Wellbeing Workshop

Meditation for Beginners

By Shelley Wilson

Published 2014, in Great Britain.

Text Copyright © Shelley Wilson 2013

Please visit
http://myresolutionchallenge.blogspot.co.uk
for contact details

ISBN: 978-1514619988

British Cataloguing Publication data:
A catalogue record of this book is available from the British Library

This book is also available as an ebook, for your kindle, ipad, ipod touch, iphone, pc, mac...

This book is dedicated to my holistic health clients and students.

Thank you for allowing me to be a part of your life journey.

Contents

Introduction

If you don't know a chakra from a chorizo, or you prefer a pair of Jimmy Choo shoes over walking barefoot on dew-covered grass, then you've come to the right place.

I teach meditation classes, not to highly spiritual students with hairy armpits and kaftans, but to ladies who are just like you and me, career women, single parents, teachers, nurses and retired grandparents. Meditation is available to everyone; you don't need to be spiritual to enjoy the benefits of this practice.

We all experience those moments when we are caught up in a whirlwind of thoughts.

When I teach meditation classes, I refer to those moments often. It's when your mind refuses to stop its internal chatter. When you have a constant stream of, 'did I put the cat out?' or 'I forgot to email x about y,' and, 'what shall we have for dinner?' I, therefore, coined the phrase 'sausage and mash moments'. We all have them but hopefully by the time you've read this guide, your sausage and mash moments will be greatly reduced.

When you first heard about meditation, what was your reaction? Maybe you thought it was a load of nonsense. Perhaps you thought it was a religious act for priests, monks or rabbis, or did you think it was a past time for hippies wearing floating robes, bamboo sandals and chanting in fields.

Meditation is, in fact, the simple task of being in the now. Living in the present and trying to be still and stop the racing thoughts that occupy our brains 24/7.

This book is designed to be your personal pocket guide to meditation. You won't need to find the extra time or buy special equipment. Using the tools and tips in this book you will learn to switch off and start on the road to a more balanced life.

Couldn't we all benefit from a bit of peace and quiet? Have you ever experienced that moment when you get up early, and everyone is asleep. You make yourself a coffee and sit in silence, maybe looking at your garden or reading the paper, but all around you is quiet. That is what meditation is all about – finding that peace, releasing any tension and relaxing.

You can meditate in your pyjamas sat on the couch, you can meditate in your business suit on the train, and you can even meditate in your jeans and jumper while sat in the dentist's chair.

Meditation is very simple – take ten minutes to read this guide and you'll see for yourself.

Benefits

Why meditate? In very simple terms, it will relax you.

How much money have you spent on feel-good products over the last twelve months, or prescription drugs for your varying illnesses? What if you could find a way to relieve those tight shoulder muscles or stop the persistent headaches? What if you could lull yourself into a restful sleep and beat insomnia, and what if all that could be done for FREE?

It sounds like a dodgy advert in the back of a magazine doesn't it. We pay out huge sums of money on gym memberships, spa breaks and beauty products and prescribed medication to try and relax and achieve the inner peace that has always resided within. It costs nothing to sit down, sigh and take a moment for you, and the benefits of doing such a simple task are well documented.

Let's take a look at just a handful of the physiological benefits of meditation:-

- It slows our heart rate down.
- It decreases respiratory rate.

- It reduces anxiety.
- All the aches, pains and tension in our muscles decreases.
- Cholesterol levels drop.
- It helps us retain our youthful looks.
- What about the psychological benefits:-
- It can boost our self-confidence.
- Our concentration is more focused.
- We are more creative.
- We have an improved memory.

The most significant benefit, of course, is that it's completely free. In other words, it's all good news, and there is nothing stopping you from giving it a go.

The Science Bit

As this book is a beginner's guide to meditation I'm not going to go all neuroscientist on you, but understanding your brain activity can help when you begin to meditate. You may start to recognise the different stages as you practice.

Brain activity tends to fall into the following four groups:-

- Beta
- Alpha
- Theta
- Delta

When we are asleep, it's the Delta waves that are dominant, and when we are awake and fully active, such as at work or the gym, then the Beta waves are strongest.

Each group may feel like this:-

- Beta = Awake and alert, fully conscious.
- Alpha = Relaxed and calm, creative and meditative, at peace.

- Theta = Deeply relaxed and problem-solving (this is the meditation state).
- Delta = Deep, dreamless sleep.

Switching from a full on exercise workout, where you are concentrating on a specific task, to a quick ten minutes in the sauna, means your brain has moved from Beta to Alpha.

If you were meditating, you would drop into a deeper relaxed state and enter Theta where your brain activity slows down to the point of nodding off.

By practising meditation, your brain is entering a more relaxed state on a regular basis that allows your body to relax, lowers your heart rate and blood pressure and reduces stress and tension.

It's not just our brain activity that changes when we meditate; we also experience a physical reaction. Our adrenal glands produce cortisol that is a stress hormone used for energy. Very useful for our caveman ancestors who needed to either fight and kill their dinner or realise when they were outnumbered and run. We refer to this as a 'fight or flight' response.

When your muscles are tense and your shoulders stiff, then your central nervous system is switched on, and you are ready for a 'fight or flight' response. Meditation switches off the stress hormone, and your body relaxes, tension melts away, and your shoulders drop to a more relaxed position.

Are You Sitting Comfortably?

Have you noticed that five or six days into any holiday your mind stops whirling, you stop wondering how many emails will greet you once you get home, and you begin to let go? It is a sure sign that your mind is relaxing and in turn your body will relax.

Relaxation is a physical thing and the body and mind are linked - when the body relaxes so does the mind and vice versa.

Meditation relaxes the mind and body, your breathing slows down, your mind switches off and your muscles relax.

To begin to experience this we need to make sure we are comfortable and our posture is conducive to good relaxation.

A perfect posture would look something like this:-

- Sitting straight
- Shoulders loose and eased back slightly
- Arms and hands floppy

- Stomach loose, don't tense the muscles just let them 'hang'
- Feet flat on the floor.

During my training, I only attempted the Lotus Position once (this is where you sit cross-legged but loop your feet through so they are resting in your lap). It was very uncomfortable on my hips and knees and I lasted all of about five seconds. The best advice I can give you is to find a position that's right for you.

If you meditate at home, choose a comfy chair with good back support, try not to meditate in bed as you will probably fall asleep and that's not meditating, that's just sleeping!

As you sit quietly, picture a piece of string coming out of the ceiling and in through the top of your head. It runs in a straight line through your body and comes out from your tail bone, through the chair, and the carpet and into the foundations of your house. While you meditate, try and keep the string steady. Now you are ready to start.

Breathing

The way in which we breathe is key to meditating. Rhythmic breathing calms the mind and body. When you breathe in the air flows through your nose, down your windpipe and into the airways in your lungs.

Slowing our breathing can help us sort through our emotions and prioritise our thoughts, but many of us don't breathe correctly. I know this sounds rather silly, you are reading this book and you are happily breathing in and out, but how well are you breathing?

Stop for a moment and picture how far each breath is going in your body. Don't take a deep breath just breathe normally. Can you feel the air flowing down your nose to the back of your throat? Does it seem to stop there, and then you have to breathe out again?

Have you ever watched children when they are asleep? Their stomachs will rise and fall with each breath, rather than their chest. They are breathing correctly.

As we get older and find a job, pay bills and settle down, we allow stress to creep into our lives. We tend to take short breaths as we are overwhelmed with decisions and our to-do lists. We are at risk of permanently hyperventilating. If we carry on breathing in this manner, it will begin to have a detrimental effect on our bodies. Insomnia, stomach disorders and depression can begin to manifest – all this from such a simple act done in the wrong way.

Try this exercise to find out if you are breathing properly:-

- Sit up straight in a sturdy chair.
- Place your left hand on your chest.
- Place your right hand just above your belly button, on your abdomen.
- Now breathe in – your left hand should remain still, and your right hand should move up and down.

If your left hand is moving then you need to alter how you breathe, your breath is too shallow. When you begin to breathe properly into your diaphragm, then only your right hand will move. You are now breathing in the right way.

By altering your breathing technique and taking slower, more rhythmic breaths it will benefit you on a physical level - fewer coughs and colds as your immunity improves and your stress levels will begin to reduce. It will also help with any exercising as your body is now receiving the correct levels of energy-giving oxygen.

To start meditating, we simply picture the journey of our breath as it travels through our body.

Try this simple exercise:-

- Close your eyes and take a deep breath.
- Begin to maintain a calm rhythm of breathing.
- Picture the air moving through your nose, down your throat and dropping to your diaphragm – this is the muscle between your chest and stomach. (If it helps, then place your hands as in the breathing exercise previously described; left hand on your chest, right hand on your abdomen).
- Picture your breath flowing down and up in a slow rhythmic pattern. Imagine it like a yo-yo on a string, uncurling as it travels through you and then bouncing back up once it reaches your diaphragm. Use whatever

method works best for you but keep the rhythm slow and steady.

One of the techniques I use in my classes is to count the in and out breath as 'one' and 'two'. It helps as you have something to focus on which will inevitably stop those sausage and mash moments.
    Try this:-

- Close your eyes and take a deep breath.
- Begin to maintain a calm rhythm of breathing.
- Now on your next breath in (inhalation) count silently, one (do it in your head).
- As you breathe out (exhalation) count...two (again do this in your head).
- Wait for the next breath and count again, one.
- Exhale, two.
- Inhale, one.
- Exhale, two.
- Carry on counting every breath in and out as one, two.
- Notice how calm and gentle your breathing becomes and how your body starts to relax.

You will find this is a perfect exercise to try if you are struggling to get to sleep.

Try and practise this for five minutes every day. I show how you can 'add' meditation into your daily life in the next chapter.

Take Five

Many people shy away from meditation because they don't think they have the time. These people are exactly the ones who should meditate. Life is so fast; we live in a world where you can be contacted 24/7.

We never switch off and our electronic gadgets ping every ten seconds with Facebook or LinkedIn updates or re-pins and tweets.

So in this crazy age, how is it possible to 'take five' and meditate to keep our morale up and our stress levels down in our day-to-day lives?

Five minutes is all you need. Surely everyone can squeeze that out of their day can't they? Let's think about your average day:-

- Get up and have breakfast.
- Take a shower.
- Drive to work/take kids to school.

I don't need to keep going because straight away I can see twenty minutes of meditation opportunities before you've even done any work or hit the shops.

Get Up

If you are anything like me the first thing you do upon waking up is run to the toilet. It's one of the most natural things in the world and yet we can be very demure about it.

There is no need to be shy; in fact if we carry on we could raise a generation of kids with bladder and urinary problems. Going to the toilet is your first chance to have five minutes to yourself – embrace it. When you sit on the toilet, let everything go and imagine all your worries emptying out of your body and take great pleasure in flushing them away. Well done, you've just done your first meditation – now go and wash your hands!

Breakfast

If you stand over the sink and slide a bowl of Weetabix down your throat every morning then STOP! Concentrate on what you are doing as you prepare your first meal of the day. Notice the shape of the bowl, the texture of the cereal, the colour of the milk. Sit at the table in a comfortable position and savour the moment. Watch your spoon as it moves toward your open mouth and savour every mouthful, recognising flavours, textures and smells. Well done, you've just done a food meditation.

Shower

Make sure the temperature is just right and step into the stream of water. Wait a moment before your start lathering and scrubbing and let the water cascade over you and wash away all your worries, see them swirling down the plughole. Take your time with the shampoo and instead of leaping from the shower once you're done, to rub yourself raw, wrap a fluffy towel around your body and leisurely brush your hair. Well done, you've just done a shower meditation.

Driving

Give yourself plenty of time to enjoy your journey. You could take an alternative route to work and take note of the new scenery. If you are stuck in traffic place your hands on your chest and abdomen and practise your diaphragm breathing. If you have to stop at the lights, concentrate on the colour until it changes. Well done, you've just done a driving meditation.

Have a think about the rest of your day and what you could achieve in five minutes, to help you relax, slow your breathing and ease your shoulders back? There are no set rules; you are free to invent your own Take Five Meditations.

Scripts and Music

As we have already discovered, meditation is the simple act of being still and quiet, whether that's sat on the toilet or counting your breathing. You don't need anything else to benefit from meditation.

Meditating in this way is the simplest. You can do it anywhere, for as long or short as you like and you don't need any equipment. Yes, it takes practise, but then doesn't everything that's worth doing?

You've also just discovered how to find pockets of time in your day for five-minute meditations.

What this chapter touches on is how music and visualisations can deepen your experience – read this and then decide for yourself if you prefer breathing exercises over focusing on music or following a visualisation script. I've included this because I see the benefits first hand in my classes and I wanted to share that with you – it's up to you if you use these techniques or not.

When I teach meditation classes, I use certain tools. I have candles, crystals and music, I read guided visualisations from a script and I have an assortment of blankets to keep my students' toes warm.

The scripts I use are like short stories. It can be a trip to a faraway beach with an ocean that stretches for miles, or flying through the stars on the living room rug. You may prefer ambling through a forest with the sound of birds and a bubbling brook in the distance. These methods are visualisation meditations. So scripts have their uses.

If the snow is falling outside, I send my students off to a warm beach so they can swim in the ocean and wiggle their toes in the sand. It's not hypnosis; visualisation meditation is simply the act of picturing what the reader is saying and following the story – a bit like an audio book. Who wouldn't have climbed on top of a giant peach if they had their eyes closed, listening to Roald Dahl?

It is possible to purchase apps or a CD with pre-recorded guided meditations. It is trial and error as to whether you will like the script or get annoyed by the voice of the reader; this is a personal choice and can get expensive as you seek that ultimate escape.

One thing I suggest to my students is to record themselves reading a script on to their phones or MP3s. They can choose what they want to hear, and there are hundreds of free scripts available online that you can use (see the Helping Hand chapter for some examples to get you started). Choose the one you like, print it off, press record as you start to read (slowly) and then relax, take a deep breath and listen back. If you don't like the sound of your voice, ask a friend whose voice relaxes you if they would let you record them instead.

The music I use to accompany my visualisations I pick up at garden centres, holistic shops or car boots. I love the sound of the sea, and this works very well as background music for beach scripts. You may like to hear birds tweeting or a waterfall; the sound of a thunderstorm and rain may be just what you need to relax.

Whether you use scripts or not, the sounds of nature can relax even the most uptight of people and so listening to the right music can in itself become your simple meditation method.

When choosing music, however, avoid the heavy rock, hip hop or chart music designed to fill a dance floor. Meditation music needs to be quiet and dreamy. Keep the volume quite low and the stereo on the other side of the room. Sit in a sturdy chair, eyes closed and your hands placed on your lap and concentrate on your breathing, and then let the music wash over you. If the rhythm is slow, try to match your breathing with the music and enjoy the relaxation.

Helping Hand

I've put together a couple of short meditations for you to use in this chapter; there is a simple grounding colour exercise and a breathing exercise. Don't forget to record yourself reading these meditations and then use the playback function to enjoy whenever and wherever you choose.

You don't have to keep these to yourself either, try and involve the family. One of my clients visits her nan every Saturday, and they close the curtains, dim the lights and listen to a meditation CD together for half an hour. It's a routine they both enjoy and a special bond to share.

Children benefit hugely from meditation techniques and are surprisingly good at it. I use meditation scripts with my children, in the same way you would read a bedtime story and I recommend them to other clients whose children are having trouble sleeping, concentrating or feeling overwhelmed with exams. A friend of mine, Jane, who is a childminder, uses a dreamy music CD to calm the children when they have had a boisterous afternoon, with stunning results.

Grounding Colour Exercise

- Sit quietly, close your eyes and take a few deep breaths.
- Imagine a bright white light entering through the top of your head.
- As it travels to your forehead, it turns into a rich indigo.
- The light travels to your throat and becomes a soft blue colour.
- It travels down your chest and turns green over your heart.
- As it travels further to your abdomen, it turns yellow.
- Just below your belly button it becomes orange.
- The light travels to the base of your spine and turns into a rich red,
- It then travels further into the ground beneath you, into the soil and deep into the earth's core and it anchors you to the very centre of the earth, keeping you grounded and safe.
- Move on to the breathing exercise if you wish or take a deep breath and carry on with your day, knowing you are balanced and ready for anything.

Breathing Exercise

- Sit in a comfortable position and take a deep breath.
- Close your eyes and relax your muscles.
- Concentrate on your breathing – notice how it flows in and out.
- Don't change how you breathe just let the breath flow.
- Notice how your body feels as your breathing gets calmer.
- When your attention wanders, which it will, simply focus back on the flow – in and out.
- Notice how deep and calm your breathing has become.
- Don't dwell on stray thoughts, let them pass.
- See the air entering in through your nose.
- See the air filling your body gently.
- Feel your stomach gently rise and fall.
- Notice the pause.
- See the air as it leaves your body.
- As you inhale count one.
- As you exhale count two.
- Continue counting every inhalation and exhalation (one, two).

- When you feel ready, notice the sounds around you.
- Wiggle your fingers and toes and shrug your shoulders gently.
- Open your eyes and slowly return to your day feeling relaxed and refreshed.

Take a look online for other resources you can use. A great site for free meditation scripts and downloads is Nigel Coates's 'Explore Meditation'

http://www.exploremeditation.com

Advanced Meditators

There are so many different ways to meditate; this book is purely a beginner's guide. It only covers the basics, but should you get struck by a bolt of inspiration, then there are plenty of websites and books for the more advanced meditator. There is a host of opportunities available to increase the relaxation and enjoyment of a meditation session.

- Using Crystals
- Meditation Retreats
- Labyrinths
- Mandalas
- Mantras

Using Crystals

Crystals have been used for thousands of years, and although scientific research can't prove that crystals have a direct effect on disease, they have discovered that crystals vibrate. Holistic health practitioners believe that crystals vibrate at different frequencies, like a tuning fork, and work with the body's vibrational system to balance blocked energy fields.

In meditation, holding a crystal in the palm of your hand can be very comforting, whether you believe in their qualities or not. I have a large celestite crystal that I pass around my class to demonstrate the vibrational qualities and even the most sceptical student is amazed to feel a throbbing sensation from the stone. Stones such as amethyst, clear quartz and turquoise are perfect to hold when meditating. Further information can be found at:

http://www.shamanscrystal.co.uk

Meditation Retreats

Many retreats are available for anyone wishing to mix a holiday with learning to meditate or advancing their skills. The retreats are normally in grand venues within beautiful grounds, providing home cooked meals and non-religious meditations, so they are universal. Some retreats offer a weekend break ideal for beginners. There is also the opportunity to delve further into meditation techniques and visit India, Tibet or Europe and immerse yourself in the teachings and practices for a week, month or longer. Further information can be found at:

http://www.thegoodretreatguide.com

Labyrinths

Labyrinths have a history dating back 4000 years, the Romans used them as floor designs and the medieval Gothic cathedrals in Europe used them. One of the most well-known can be found at Chartres Cathedral in France. There are many myths and legends associated with labyrinths, and they make for good reading if you do wish to delve a little deeper.

Unlike a maze, which has one way in and one way out, a labyrinth has only one path that winds through to the very centre.

For meditation purposes, you walk along the single path, concentrating on your journey until you find the centre. Once there, you can sit quietly and contemplate life, the weather or whatever takes your fancy, before starting the journey back.

Further information can be found at:

http://www.labyrinthsociety.org

Mandalas

Imagery is a wonderful tool that can be used in meditation and one of my students' favourite topics is the use of a Mandala. The word Mandala means 'circle' in Sanskrit and these symbols are used for art therapy, prayer and meditation.

This simple circle can represent the universe, creation or a life cycle depending on your interpretation. The Mandalas I use are blank, and my students colour them in at home as a way to relax. We then use the finished Mandalas to focus on during meditation, concentrating on the shapes and the colours. Further information can be found at:

http://www.mandalaproject.org

Mantras

Sound repetition is one of the simplest forms of meditation. Mantras can be a word, phrase, sound or a syllable. They are powerful when said aloud but are just as effective when repeated silently in your mind. Give this one a try – sitting in a comfortable position, eyes closed and hands placed in your lap, say out loud OM (pronounced AUM) – SHANTI – OM. Repeat this three times.

You will feel the vibrations in your body; they are working to balance your energies. 'OM' means Absolute Infinity and 'Shanti' means Peace and Tranquillity.

An affirmation, or repetition of a phrase, works just as well. Try this – 'I am happy and content.' Repeat this as many times as you wish.

The queen of affirmations is Louise Hay, find out more about her work at:

http://www.louisehay.com

Conclusion

I hope you enjoyed this pocket guide to meditation. As a regular meditator and workshop tutor, I experience the benefits of meditation first hand, but as a single mum to three teens I also understand how life can take over. It is far too easy to leave your wellbeing behind as you look out for everyone else.

This book gives you a starting point to focus on; it's there to remind you that you DO have time in your busy schedule; you ARE worth it and you CAN meditate.

Reinforce your learning and tell five people today what you've learnt from this book. Give them the same tools you now possess to fit a five-minute meditation in before that next meeting or before the school run.

Most of all – have fun and enjoy your new found relaxation time.

Happy Meditating

Other Books by This Author

Thank you for purchasing this book, if you loved reading it as much as I loved writing it then, please spread the meditation joy and recommend this guide to a friend. Leaving a review on Amazon helps others to find out the benefits of meditation.

In the meantime you might like to check out some of my other titles:

How I Changed My Life In a Year:
One Woman's Mission To Lose Weight, Get Fit, Beat Her Demons, And Find Happiness
...In Twelve Easy Steps!
(Non-Fiction)

Vision Boards For Beginners
Part of the 'Wellbeing Workshop' series
(Non-Fiction)

Guardians Of The Dead
Book 1 of 'The Guardians' series
(Young-Adult Fiction)

About the Author

Shelley Wilson divides her writing time between motivational non-fiction for adults and the fantasy worlds of her young adult fiction.

Shelley's books combine lifestyle, motivation and self-help with a healthy dose of humour. She works in the Mind, Body, Spirit sector as a practitioner and tutor. Her approach to writing is to provide an uplifting insight into personal development and being the best you can be.

Shelley writes her Young Adult Fiction under 'S.L Wilson' and combines myth, legend and fairy tales with a side order of demonic chaos. You can find all her books on amazon.

She was born in Yorkshire but raised in Solihull, England. Don't be fooled by the smile - she has a dark side and exercises her right to be mischievous on a regular basis. She is an obsessive list maker, social media addict and a huge Game of Thrones fan.

You can connect with Shelley online, via the following websites:-

Blog: http://myresolutionchallenge.blogspot.com

Facebook:
http://www.facebook.com/resolutionchallenge

Website: http://shelleywilsonauthor.com

Twitter: http://www.twitter.com/ShelleyWilson72

Acknowledgments

I want to take this opportunity to thank the many people who have helped me put together my Wellbeing Workshop Series. Writing is such a solitary profession, but I am so lucky to have a great team working with me. Huge thanks go to Peter Jones, from Soundhaven Books, for the incredible cover art, and thanks also to Rebecca, my lovely proofreader for this series.

My thank you list wouldn't be complete without a mention for my meditation class students. I wouldn't be where I am today without your support, love and friendship.

Thanks to my close friends and family. You guys are behind me one hundred percent in everything I do, and I love you all so much.

And of course, to my three beautiful children, you are my inspiration, my life and my best friends – I love you all to the moon and back.